D0301825

فلسطين حبيبتي

FOR PALESTINE

FOR PALESTINE

LEENA SARASTE

translated by

GREG COOGAN

ZED BOOKS LTD.

For Palestine was first published in Finnish under the title *Rakkaani Palestiina* by Tutkijaliitto, Helsinki in 1983; in English by Zed Books Ltd., 57 Caledonian Road, London N1 9BU, in 1985.

Designed by Tapio Vapaasalo

Translated from the Finnish by Greg Coogan

Printed in Finland by Forssan Kirjapaino Oy

Typeset by Graffiti Oy

British Library Cataloguing in Publication Data

Saraste, Leena
For Palestine
1.Lebanon—History—Israeli intervention
I. Title II. Rakkaani, Palestiina.
English
956.92'044 DS87.53

ISBN 0-86232-413-0
ISBN 0-86232-414-9Pb

US Distributor:
Biblio Distribution Centre, 81 Adams Drive,
Totowa, New Jersey 07512, USA.

Contents

We shall never leave

...
Here
On your breasts
We persist
like a wall
In your throats
as broken glass
unshakeable
And in your eyes
as a tempest of fire

Here
on your breasts
We persist
like a wall
To wash your dishes in your dives
To fill gentlemen's glasses
To scrub the tiles in the black kitchens
To grab a mouthful
for our little ones
From your blue fangs

Here
On your breasts
We persist
like a wall
Starving
naked
provocative
reciting poems

We are the guardians of the shade
Of orange trees and olive trees
We sow ideas like yeast in the pastry
Our nerves are of ice
But our hearts blaze with fire
If we are thirsty
we shall wring the stones
We shall eat dirt
if we are hungry
BUT WE SHALL NEVER LEAVE
And we shall never begrudge our blood

Here
We have a past
a present

Here
Is our future...

TAWFIK ZAYYAD 1965

Looking for Palestine

"Here we persist," says Tawfik Zayyad in his poem. "We" are the Palestinians. "Here" is their country, Palestine.

Palestine?

I had a strange feeling the first time I set out to visit a Palestinian refugee camp. I wondered just where I was going. I knew it was not Palestine, a country that as a child I had had vague dreams of seeing. It had still been on the world map when I started school; then it simply vanished, and was heard of no more. But the Palestinians themselves certainly remained in the news. And in recent years they — now numbering some five million — have been featured in increasingly tragic reports with growing frequency.

We have been told how a persecuted homeless people, the Jews, were given an uninhabited country, the promised land Palestine, to settle. The Bible tells us how bloody the conquest of that promised land was thousands of years ago — and how densely inhabited it already was (see, for example, the Book of Samuel). The mass media have given us a modern version of how the land was "cleared". The Zionists have used a metaphorical comparison: to them the land was a beautiful bride, but they did not want the dowry, the people, that came with it.

Many Jews were shocked to discover that their new national homeland was not lying empty, waiting for them to make the desert bloom. Where they had expected an empty wilderness, they found people who had been cultivating their olive and orange groves for centuries, some of them even for millennia; people, nations, intermingled or in their own distinct groups. Among them was even a small Jewish population. Why could this parallel existence not continue? Why did the Palestinians leave their homes?

From Lydda to Gaza, Cairo to Beirut

"Why did you leave?" I asked Ismail Shammout, a well-known Palestinian artist. His story was the first I heard, but I was later to hear many others like it:

"When the British ruled Palestine as a mandated territory, we were used to frequent searches of our homes: there had been rebellions and insurrections against this extension of colonial rule. These searches became even more frequent as the mandate period was drawing to a close. On one occasion, the people of the town of Lydda were driven out of their homes and into the square. We were expecting to return in the evening, as we had done before, but this time the new masters marched us out of the town, at gunpoint. We could take nothing with us; our houses were left abandoned, with all our belongings in them. On the way, we were not allowed even to stop at wells to get water. Some of the old people and children succumbed to thirst and exhaustion. We even tried to chew grass to get some moisture. The march went on and on southwards, until we came to the Gaza district.

"We lived in tents the first winter: I remember my old father beside a coal brazier on a cold, damp winter's day, a scene that I have painted. My father was still living in Gaza in 1967 when the Israelis seized it, too, and a couple of years later he was able to visit his former home from there.

1
Jerusalem, the city sacred to three of the world's major religions, as depicted by a traveller, J.D. Woodward, in the 1870s.

"The house was still standing, and the whole distance of years disappeared from my father's mind. The only thing that he regretted was that one window had been bricked up; it had commanded such a beautiful view of the landscape in the evening. The Moroccan Jewish family to which the house had been given cried with my father in shared homesickness. They had been enticed to sell their house in Morocco and come to Israel, where they had not found happiness."

From Jaffa to Beirut

Tamam al-Akhal, also an artist and Ismail Shammout's wife, was thirteen when the bombs began to fall on Jaffa. The UN had piously hoped that the city would remain Palestinian, but the Israelis were unwilling to leave such an enclave in the land that they had acquired. More or less the entire population of the city had to crowd into ships and boats to escape the bombing.

Tamam told me that in the pain of departure she had carved her name on a pillar in the hallway of the house. She described the whole house in detail and asked me to visit it if I went to Jaffa. All the furniture had been left behind as well. She told me that the new occupant of the house was an artist — also a woman — who had emigrated from Germany.

Imprisonment and torture

Hussein was put in prison when he was only fourteen. He was there for a year. "I was tortured only a little, because I was so young and they knew what I had done". Together with several other boys, he had been involved in resistance activities and planned an attack on the occupying garrison. The group had decided to discontinue their studies and postpone their plans for careers as researchers and poets until their country was free. A year in prison for a child inspired by dreams and romantic patriotism? He had to go abroad to be able to study; to all intents and purposes, Israel's universities are closed to Palestinians.

There was no returning to his home, parents, brothers and sisters. Under torture, some of his comrades had stated that he was still active in a Palestinian organization banned by the Israelis. That could have earned him a ten-year sentence.

"If you go there, bring me back a little sand from the beach near my home, moistened by the sea!"

And I did, eventually, after carrying it with me through many countries to the amazement of customs officials. A little bit of Palestinian sand moistened by the water of the Mediterranean.

Sand, memories, cherished objects; when a person has become accustomed to losing everything continually, he is no longer able to cling to anything and voluntarily gives up little things when he has had to part with big things. Hussein left the sand behind in Beirut, another place that he had grown to love; he also left behind many metres of shelves filled with books of poetry, history, philosophy. How would he have taken them with him, and where?

A temporary departure — permanent exile

It is true, in a way, that some of the Palestinians left "voluntarily". Wishing to escape the terror

2
The Palestinian city of Jaffa in the 1870s. J.D. Woodward.

3
On the first day of the evacution, Tamam al-Akhal's workmates gathered at her parents' home to say goodbye. Her own home had been badly damaged in the bombing.

4
Leaving their own country did not ensure peace for the Palestinians. The war followed them to their new homelands, and also afflicted the local inhabitants. It has been decades since the farmers of South Lebanon have been able to look forward to harvesting their crops in peace. The Beaufort mountaintop fortress provides little protection in modern warfare.

2

3

4

raging all around them, they fled to neighbouring countries to wait for the situation to calm down and allow them to return to their homes. There was time to lock up their barns and they took the keys with them: these large iron keys now sometimes hang in places of honour in refugee homes.

Those who fled their homes to escape the terror of 1948 have not yet been permitted to return to Palestine, but the descendants of Jews who left thousands of years ago and their co-religionists are welcomed home, to Israel.

The Palestinian refugee camps are located outside Israel, both in neighbouring Arab countries and in the Gaza and West Bank areas, which were occupied by Israel in 1967. Camps and villages often blend into each other, but the camps are newer and of much inferior construction, hastily erected. The lushness of the neatly cultivated fields and gardens in and around the camps and villages shows that the inhabitants are rooted in the soil, although many of them have several times seen the patches of land their ancestors cultivated violently seized by Israel.

Umm Khalil, still in Palestine

To be able to remain in his homeland, a person needs dignity and work, a livelihood.

"In Jerusalem I saw women in a queue waiting for their refugee rations, flour distributed by the United Nations Relief and Works Agency (UNRWA), outside the organization's building. It felt bitter. I rebelled: why does the UN not help us to return to our homes, to get back our fields instead of giving us those inadequate little tokens of charity? Why doesn't Europe help: can it not see the situation? Why doesn't anybody help? But then I asked myself: 'why don't we help ourselves, why don't I help?' " Umm Khalil, the chairperson of the In'ash El-Usra Palestinian women's organization, recognized the humiliation of being a refugee. For people to be able to help themselves they need education and training. To be able to avail themselves of that they need money for food. Nobody can learn when he is hungry.

Umm Khalil's organization runs a school with a broad and varied curriculum that concentrates particularly on traditional women's occupations. The school must support itself, because the Israeli authorities have banned cash collections on security grounds. The same reasons have been invoked to ban Umm Khalil from leaving the town of al-Bireh, where she lives and works. She was refused permission even to bury her husband in his home town. She has been imprisoned five times for her outspoken comments. Virtually every Palestinian who has played an active role has been detained at least once, but few have been given a trial. Neither prison nor house arrest scare them, but the threat of deportation does. That silences people and often discourages them from working actively for their national cause.

The school has made it possible for many families to earn a livelihood and stay in their home country. From a small sewing course for eight girls, started with the help of a loan from the mayor, since deported, Umm Khalil's project has grown into an impressive establishment that gives training in traditional handicrafts as well. The building contains sales showrooms, to which 2,000 women from the surrounding villages bring what they have made each month. This provides about 50% of their families' incomes. In the same

5
Even in the occupied areas and in spite of all the difficulties that afflict them, the Palestinian organizations have managed to improve the position of women by giving them education and training. Men still learn trades from their parents, unless they travel abroad to study, even at the risk of not being allowed to return. This picture shows a carpenter's shop in a refugee camp in the Gaza Strip.

6
Children grow up in the midst of war and become accustomed to destruction. The Rashidiyeh camp near the Israeli border had suffered repeated bombing raids for years before the war in the summer of 1982 and the occupation that followed.

7
The people who have remained in Palestine proudly cherish their traditions. Women always embroider new dresses to replace their old ones that have been worn threadbare. Members of the younger generation do not always master this skill; working for a living forces people to be practical and traditional garments are worn only on festive occasions. Gaza, 1982.

5

6

7

8
The UNRWA seeks to provide every child in the Palestinian refugee camps with ten years of basic schooling, but the constant state of war causes many interruptions. This picture was taken in the Kabul School in the Shatila camp in 1980. School satchels full of explosives were found in the schoolyard on several occasions in the winter of 1983.

9
Security precautions made it impossible to photograph more extensive views. The surroundings of the Ain al-Helweh school fascinated me and I planned to return and photograph the view when the situation calmed down. I was only given permission to photograph when there was nothing more to lose. The school had been bombed and its ruins bulldozed. All that remained on the site were tents. February 1983.

10
Everything that the small Palestinian clinic in Hebron could do was being done to save seven-months-old Amira, who weighed only 3.2 kilogrammes. There was no room for her, nor for any of her kind, in the state hospital. Infant mortality remains high in the Israeli-occupied areas and the Palestinians are denied permission to build their own hospitals, although the money is available and the drawings ready. Providing maternity services for a population of over a million on an almost entirely voluntary basis sounds a hopeless task in such circumstances.

11
Beaufort Castle in South Lebanon dates from the time of the Crusades and had the reputation of being

building is a small museum collection and upstairs the editorial offices of the magazine *The Palestinian National Heritage*, which is supposed to appear quarterly. However, Israeli censorship — which is always in force, even in peacetime — has delayed publication of every issue, sometimes by well over a year.

A literacy campaign is run in conjunction with the handicrafts project. "The occupiers, both past and present, have been unwilling to give our people the opportunity to learn about our own history. The ignorant are humble. A similar campaign to promote literacy and revive handicraft traditions was getting under way in the camps in Lebanon just before the latest war began in 1982. The Palestinians are the best educated of all the Arab peoples, but it is futile merely to point to the large number of individuals with academic degrees if at the same time a section of the population lacks basic education and skills and languishes under oppression. Difficult conditions are an explanation, but no justification for the deprivations we suffer. Everybody independent! The country independent!" says Umm Khalil.

Over three decades in refugee camps

Why are the Palestinians not integrated in the countries they have moved to? Why do the Arab countries not do something to solve the refugee problem? Why do the Palestinians still live in refugee camps? Those are questions that are often asked.

A growing proportion of the Palestinians have acquired advanced education and professional skills, and are thus in a position to buy or rent an apartment on the open market. But a feeling of national identity and a desire to preserve their own language, or the Palestinian dialect of Arabic, as well as close family and community ties make many people, even those who have been away for years, want to come back to the camps to live. At first, the people with least hope of ever leaving the camps were those lacking the skills to adapt to new conditions, i.e. peasants. Whole village communities re-formed in the camps and clung to the old ways and attitudes, although now they lived in tents instead of houses.

The tents were gradually replaced by permanent structures. Some people found casual employment on farms in the surrounding district. Others went to work in the Gulf countries to earn the money to support their often numerous relatives. This took the family off the UNRWA refugee lists and removed what little aid they had been receiving. UNRWA-run schools were set up in the camps. Gradually, the Palestinian organizations set up their own clinics, hospitals, maternity care services and workshops, and thus became self-sufficient.

The little houses that have sprouted from the original tents climb towards the sky; the only direction in which there is room to grow is up. Habitations originally intended to be temporary soon became too small for the growing families that lived in them. More room was needed for the new generation. So the camps grew and blended with the surrounding towns and cities; became suburbs. Sewer systems, water mains and improvised electricity distribution systems were developed and continued to function until the Israeli invasion in June 1982. The fruit trees in the small courtyards had already grown higher than

8

9

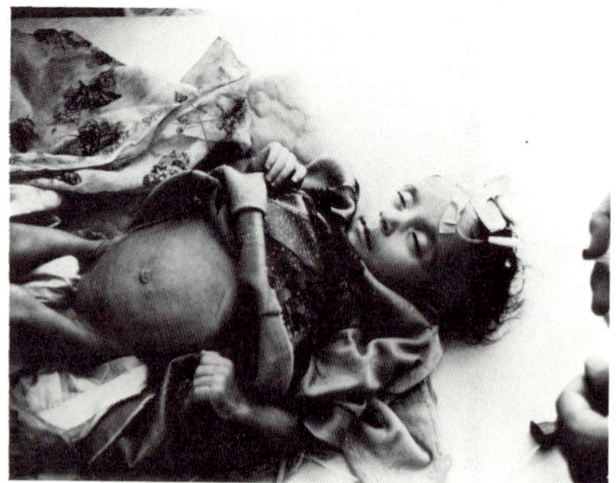
10

11

the walls: vines yielded their grapes and gave shade from the searing sun. Sage and thyme, and sometimes even olive trees, grew in pots and jars, to be taken home when the time was ripe.

The UN's resolutions and promises of a return to the people's own home proved empty. There has been no word about when this will materialize. Now even the camps have been destroyed, and reconstruction is not permitted. Over 90% of the largest Palestinian refugee camp in Lebanon, Ain al-Helweh, has been destroyed. Some 70% of Rashidiyeh was destroyed right at the beginning of the invasion. In the camps in the Beirut area, Sabra, Shatila and Burj al-Barajneh, the destruction is still going on.

The losers' town

The town of Damour lies 20 kilometres south of Beirut, just outside the area protected by the city's anti-aircraft system. Its location on the coast and the main highway to the south gives it major strategic importance. It has been the target of repeated Israeli bombing raids.

In October 1980, I watched from the balcony of my hotel as enormous columns of smoke from bombs dropped by four Phantom jets rose into the sky. While this was going on, a radio broadcast was proclaiming that it was not a retaliatory strike: "Now we have taken the initiative," said the Israeli announcer. In July 1981, the town was bombed 11 times. Less than a year later, in the early days of the war, it was completely destroyed and its inhabitants forced to flee, many of them for the fourth time in their lives.

The town looked idyllic, until one noticed how damaged the buildings were. In the summer of 1982, every house had been occupied. Gardens were tended with loving care. For many Palestinians, it was the first chance since leaving their homeland to test their skills at growing lettuce, tomatoes and fruit. The town soon achieved self-sufficiency and later was able to add diversity to the food supply of the whole surrounding district.

Damour's new residents had come there in 1976. It had originally had a prosperous Lebanese population and remained fairly quiet during the Lebanese civil war, until the Falangist Christians cut the supply route to the South. In the battle that ensued, the Muslims managed to gain control of the whole town and evacuated the population. They then moved in survivors of a massacre carried out by the Falangists in East Beirut's Karantina Muslim enclave. About half the survivors from the Tall al-Zaatar siege were moved in later. The new inhabitants of the town were in such poor condition after their ordeal that they were not able to repair the buildings. At first, they lived in very crowded conditions, often several families to a dwelling, but gradually they began to improve the state of the town and tend the gardens and orchards there. The houses were large, but had been severely damaged in the war. There was not a single window intact. The glass was replaced with plastic sheeting; continual explosions do not damage this material.

I found the town very charming and always looked at it when I drove past on the highway. One Saturday in April 1982, just before the invasion, I was given permission to visit it. Mohammed agreed to take me to spend the night with his sister's family.

Arriving at Miriam's house in the dark was an experience. A fragrance in the air indicated that

impregnable. It had been bombed repeatedly for years, but withstood all assaults. Suddenly in June 1982, it was overwhelmed by the Israelis after only a brief battle. Why? One explanation is that the Israelis used poison gas or a chemical that asphyxiated the defenders. The defenders numbered about thirty. I knew one of them, 17-year-old Nabil, who was in Beirut in April that year to have an artificial limb fitted. He had lost his leg in bombing the previous year. "The new leg is a lot better; it is made of steel," said the boy. Where might he be now?

12
The scenes of destruction in Shatila were partly hidden in the shadows of the spreading stone pines. It was in the shade of the same trees that the massacre began. The area was later patrolled by Italian and French soldiers, but they, too, have since departed and the destruction goes on.

13 and 14
When the original inhabitants of Damour left the town, they felled as many fruit trees as they had time to.

12

13

But many remained, and the soil in the courtyards of the houses that the new settlers, land-hungry Palestinians and Lebanese, moved into was rich and fertile.

15
Children learn at an early age to look after each other. Big sister Nadja, who is only 10, prepares breakfast, which is eaten outdoors most of the year. Nadja serves tea with cheese and olives wrapped in thin sheets of bread. Damour, April 1982.

16
I was in the grip of an unpleasant premonition when I entered Damour in April 1982, but my fear eased as soon as my taxi stopped. Four men, their arms full of explosives that had just been found in a car, rushed past. Car bombs often come in pairs. Everybody is relieved when one is discovered before it explodes, but sometimes it lulls them into a false sense of security and the other one takes a terrible toll.

17
In winter, one can try to keep a tent warm with the aid of a kerosene heater, but in such a crowded space it is dangerous. 47-year-old Zeynab is feeding her granddaughter Mervat. Behind her are her own daughters: 12-year-old Miriam and 13-year-old Ibtissam, who has been mute since the horrors of Tall al-Zaatar.

there were lemon trees in the courtyard. As we stumbled into the house, the children woke up; little heads began rising from the mattresses laid out side-by-side on the floor. The next day was Sunday, so the bedtime rules were not so important. The children watched television while we admired the new baby in the house, five-days-old Jasmine, whose tightly bundled little body was passed from lap to lap. She was the tenth child to be born into the family, and it was not by any means certain that she would be the last. Little Mohammed had starved to death in Tall al-Zaatar, and Zuheila had been shot in the stomach. The death of a child makes one feel that there is nothing to justify preventing the birth of even a single baby. Their house was large; there was plenty of floor space for more beds. But Damour was destroyed. I heard in August that the family had survived and made its way to Baalbek.

Leaving home a third time

Some of the families in Damour were now living in tents for the third time in their lives. Many of them had left Galilee or other northern parts of Palestine in 1948 and eventually ended up on the eastern outskirts of Beirut where they built a camp they called Tall al-Zaatar. It means "Thyme Hill".

The change from living in a tent to a permanent building meant a slight improvement in the standard of comfort enjoyed by a family. It also meant enormous financial sacrifices and sharp economies in the large family's spending. To improve the family's finances, the men went abroad in search of work. Hassan and his wife Zeynab took all 17 children with them to Germany for a couple of years; all of them can still speak a few words of German. It was homesickness that brought them back again; kith and kin make even a refugee camp a home. Now the family, with the eight youngest children, lives in the al-Sitt Zeynab tent camp near Damascus in Syria. The tents there are 4 × 4 metres in size and provide little protection against either the cold of winter or the heat of summer. Even a sigh can be heard next door.

Zeynab's friends and daughters-in-law like to come visiting. Like all Palestinians, she is hospitable. Misfortune is also a strong binding force. Two of the family's children were killed in the fighting, and a third has been missing since the Shatila massacre. Three lost their power of speech in the horror of Tall al-Zaatar. The mother of the neighbouring family has not spoken since the end of the siege, either, except sometimes "Oh my God, oh my God!" The Falangists murdered her ten-year-old son and forced her to tread on his face.

The future is hope, the present a nightmare

I tried to learn to understand what makes people endure, believe that justice will triumph in spite of everything, keep believing that there will be a return to their homeland.

"If not us, then our descendants, our great-great-great grandchildren, or their children, will go back. After all not even the state established by earlier invaders, the Crusaders, lasted any longer than a century..."

The horrors of war and great sorrows are occasionally overshadowed by lesser everyday problems. How to keep the family clean and

14

16

15

17

healthy without water; how to cope with meals when one has little or no money, in a town where the ovens have been destroyed, or if they are still intact, there is no fuel with which to bake bread. Bread is a staple in the Palestinian diet, much more important than it is in Europe.

Three weeks or so after my return to Finland, I began to have nightmares, as I had had after every visit to the Middle East. I needed a secure environment in which to be able to dare to think about the horror of what I had seen. But where have the Palestinians the secure surroundings that they need to be able to release the fear that haunts them, if only through nightmares? Families have been broken up and scattered once again, and normal security is nowhere in sight; there is not even the comfort that members of the same family can give each other. Now everybody is constantly worried about loved ones far away. Being together, even when the bombs are falling, is better than being apart. A Palestinian in Europe may be in safety, but is constantly plagued by fear for the other members of the family. In the camps, one can at least find out what has happened and who has survived as soon as an air raid or artillery bombardment has ended.

During the Israeli siege of Beirut, people's will to live and ingenuity triumphed over the inhumanity of the war machine. Groups of voluntary workers took care of all practical matters and even fought in defence of the city. And Palestinian fruit began flowing into the city in spite of the siege. The availability, for the first time in over 30 years, of the famous juicy grapes that grow in the al-Khalil (Hebron) district of the West Bank, helped enormously to boost morale, as did the fact that beer and soft drinks were somehow always served cold. In the intervals between the heaviest bombardments, sheep and cattle were driven into the city; fresh meat was available every day. Prices did not rise much, either. The Lebanese smugglers were not inspired by the profit motive, but by a desire to defend life and confound the enemy, earning a moderate livelihood for themselves in the process, of course.

The agony of the evacuation

It was difficult to get around the city after the evacuation had been decided on. Everybody stopped in the streets to talk and exchange news: who was going where. The salty taste of goodbyes grew more intense. The centre of Beirut was like a small village, where one bumped into acquaintances at every turn. People had crowded into a few hotel areas that were considered relatively safe.

I was sitting in the restaurant of the Hotel Napoleon with Marjaleena Oraby, a Finnish nurse, and her husband Abdel Rahman, as well as some Palestinian friends. As we waited for the meal, I wrote in my diary. We were all tired and speaking was difficult:

Hussein is being evacuated tomorrow, Hamdi the day after. Is the sea route to Tartous safe? Day after day, those awaiting evacuation have managed to get postponements, now there is silence at every table. One's heart stops; it is difficult to breathe. People open their beer cans in unison. There are electric lights burning everywhere, the lifts work, and the water flows in the pipes. It has been possible to wash, and there has been no need for candles. The hum of generators has stopped. Medical teams sent by the churches and the others not being evacuated murmur among themselves. As always, the service

18
On Monday morning, 30 August 1983, the leadership of the Lebanese democratic movement assembled to bid farewell to the landless, respected statesman who was leaving the country. And representatives of the world media struggled for a good vantage point.

19
This meeting in Shatila blended the joy of reunion with memories of what had been lost. Umm Abdullah had arrived from Damour already in the summer. Marjaleena Oraby returned from Finland as soon as possible. A personal loss, the death of her husband in the September massacre, merely strengthened her resolve to go on working in a Palestinian hospital.

18

19

is slow — can it only be because of the war? Where there was once a window there is now a shutter of unplaned wood; those window panes still intact are criss-crossed by broad strips of brown tape. Rose-red spots flash across the darkening sky; somebody is shooting into the air.

We, the foreigners, are staying behind. But the city is emptying; what joy there was, disappearing. Once again, everybody is losing somebody, everybody faces an uncertain future. Scattering people even further like this will not solve the problem. Perhaps it will give birth to new strength, but at what cost in suffering. And those remaining behind, the families still in the camps, are preparing for an attack by the forces of the new president. A new bloodbath, a new civil war, a new Black September on the way?

The evacuation was a tremendous spectacle, a triumphant departure with flags, weapons and all the media present. Even those who had never before held a weapon wanted to fire into the air, to empty Kalashnikov magazines into the sky. The defeaning din began on the first morning of the evacuation and was interrupted only when Arafat left, an event that was honoured with silence until the roar of cannons announced that the Chairman had entered the port area. Then the noise became unbridled; the din of volleys fired close to one's ear weakens the knees and drains one's strength like an uncontrolled fit of crying. The shooting was an expression of emotion, but also a security precaution. Nobody wanted to leave ammunition behind to be confiscated, because it might well be used against their own families.

Later, every evacuee I met asked me for pictures of the bloodbath. To see if any of their relations were among the slain? To free themselves of the uncertainty?

The focus of life

Back in the tranquility of the Finnish countryside, a cuckoo calls across the lake, promising long life. Is it reminding us of our duty to stay alive. A Palestinian friend said to me in February: "You do not have the right to die." He said it angrily and convincingly. For several days he had believed that I had been killed along with his colleagues when the Palestinian Research Centre in Beirut was devastated in a bomb blast.

No right to die? Is it important in the insecurity of a refugee's life that he has friends, people to relate to, in a peaceful northern country, somebody who has a good chance of experiencing old age before life ends? Or does it seem unjust that the enemy also strikes against their friends, those who want to help by telling the world about their plight? Perhaps they cannot afford to lose a single friend, but instead all of us have a duty to live and tell others what is happening. Indeed, we can even have some effect. The smallest stone breaks the surface of calm water, and the circles spread. Information, too, spreads and influences people. I, at least, believe so, because I know it has influenced me.

We foreign friends are a fixed point on which the Palestinians can focus their lives. But there is a much stronger anchor, a country called Palestine, which can never be really lost.

Helsinki 24.5.1983

Kaana Castrén

20

THE BEIRUT CAMPS

Sabra, Shatila, Burj al-Barajneh,
meandering alleys without street names,
glowing colours, strange music.
Hospitable people show us their little homes,
which grow upwards.
Sometimes a blue painted hand beside the doorway
wards off evil.

A,C,D *Burj al-Barajneh, October 1980*
B *Shatila, October 1980*
E *Shatila-Ghobeiri, April 1982*
F *Burj al-Barajneh, April 1982*

A

B

C

E

F

A

A

B

C

A, C, D	*Burj al-Barajneh, April 1982*
B	*Burj al-Barajneh, October 1980*
E	*Sabra, October 1980*

E

D

 Shatila, October 1980

A

A,B Burj al-Barajneh, October 1980

آه يا جرحي المكابر
وطني ليس حقيبة
وأنا لستُ مسافر
إنني العاشق والأرض حبيبة
محمود درويش

THE MARTYRS' GRAVEYARD, BEIRUT, 1980

As the sun rises, the smoke of herbs,
the fragrance of cut palm leaves,
strong coffee and stone pine resin.
Dirges and readings from the Quran.
The month of fasting, Ramadan, has ended,
the three-day festival can begin.

Beirut, 1980

But why can the war not leave even the graves in peace?

FRANCE LAIT

SOUTH LEBANON, 1980

There were still some things left intact then.
South Lebanon, bombed for decades.
The town of Nabatiyeh,
Tyre and Sidon,
and close to Tyre Rashidiyeh, the refugee camp that was home to 8,000 people.
A small garden in every courtyard.
Now
the women live in the ruins, with the children.
Where have the men been taken?
Now and then one still hears shots.
Do you still remember how it was before, and even earlier,
at home, in Palestine?

All I ask

I ask nothing more
Than to die in my country,
To dissolve and merge with the soil,
To nurture the grass,
To give life to a flower
That a child of my country will pick.
All I ask
Is to remain in the bosom of my country,
As soil,
Grass,
A flower.

FADWA TOUQAN

كفانى

كفانى اظلُّ بحضنها

كفانى أَموت على أرضها
وأُدفنَ فيها
وتحت ثراها اذوب وأفنى
وأُبعثُ عشبا على أرضها
وابعث زهرة
تعبث بها كفُّ طفلٍ نَمَتْهُ بلادى
كفانى اظل بحضن بلادى
ترابا
وعشبا
وزهرة

فدوى طوقان

A

B

A, B, C, E Rashidiyeh, October 1980
D Tyre

D

C

E

 Rashidiyeh, October 1980

A

B

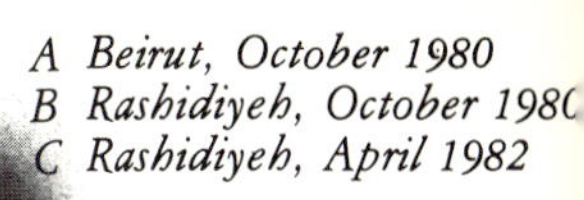
A *Beirut, October 1980*
B *Rashidiyeh, October 1980*
C *Rashidiyeh, April 1982*

C

 Rashidiyeh, October 1980

Rashidiyeh, Rashidiyeh...

Refugee camp — beloved village

The memory of the Rashidiyeh refugee camp that has remained strongest in my mind resembles a frozen photograph, which I still look at years later. The camp is quiet; it is still early morning. The Mediterranean glistens in the background. There are flowers and trees everywhere. Honeysuckle and roses fill the air with their fragrance. Orange groves, cypress-lined avenues and orchards surround the camp.

The first to wake are the roosters. From then on we hear their crowing every morning. Loudspeakers on the minaret proclaim: "Allahu akbar" — "God is great". A village of 8,000 Palestinians arises from its slumber and is soon alive with the sound of voices.

Old men dressed in traditional Arab garb and keffiyehs, plain or patterned white scarves, begin slowly moving about in the courtyards and alleys. They look at the cars collecting people going to work in the nearby town of Tyre. Little girls have gathered around the water pump to wash yesterday evening's dishes, and they chatter brightly like children anywhere.

The women stay in the camp. They look after the children and neighbours who live alone, tidy up, wash clothes and bake bread. Every minute of the day is filled with work, because feeding and looking after a large family with the aid of only rudimentary equipment is very time-consuming. Their only knowledge of the easy life is through the blue world depicted in the films on their TV sets.

Hospitable homes

Wherever we go we are followed by a crowd of children, who shout, sometimes in Arabic and sometimes in English: "Yalla! Yalla! Come!... Let's go!" Or, when they see a camera: "Sura! Sura! ... Take a picture!" Some give the victory sign, and their expressions always become serious when they do. "What is your name?" is shouted from every direction.

The older people watched us cautiously from their doors, but soon they, too, nodded and called out in friendly voices: "Ahlayn! ... Welcome" — and invited us in for coffee. A foreigner is an unaccustomed sight. For more than 30 years the camp has lived its own isolated existence, women and children rarely go outside it, and even the men only to go to work. I felt a pang in my heart and thought how privileged we were that we could come and go whenever we wanted.

A temporary state of affairs

These people have no other place besides this camp. Palestine, the homeland that they had to leave in 1948, is 17 kilometres away.

Life in a refugee camp is crowded and intensive, and one is never alone. The concrete houses in Rashidiyeh are packed

A

tightly together. An open drain flows down the middle of the narrow alley. The searingly hot sun takes care of its hygiene.

The camp is governed by a popular committee, which is a cross between a village council and a municipal corporation. It comprises ten representatives of various organizations, who are chosen in popular elections, as well as the *mukhtar*, the village elder. The committee is responsible for everyday life in the camp: schools, health care, civil defence, and also functions as the local court of justice.

Some fortunate people have been able to rent a plot of land near the camp. But neither a small plot, sage plants growing in food cans nor the vines that shade the courtyard can compensate for a lost homeland and one's own familiar fields.

Viewed from a distance, nevertheless, things looked rather good. But everything was overshadowed — and still is — by uncertainty and worry about the future. Perhaps the next attack will be tomorrow night. Martyrs' pictures pasted to the walls are a constant reminder that death is always lurking. The scars of continual bombing raids are visible everywhere. Many buildings are deserted.

Israeli planes flew over the camp every day. If they were recognized as reconnaissance aircraft, everybody calmed down. But the small, fast, low-flying fighter-bombers are feared, because nobody has time even to get into the air raid shelter before the first bombs fall.

The first occupation of Rashidiyeh

In March 1978, Israeli infantry and armour, supported by aircraft and gunboats, stormed north across the Lebanese border. The camp was heavily bombarded. Along with 300,000 Palestinians and Lebanese, the population of Rashidiyeh fled north, some of them as far as Beirut. They found shelter in temporary tent villages or in bombed or uncompleted houses.

Some 8,000 of the nearly 20,000 people who had lived in Rashidiyeh returned to the camp. Some families remained in Beirut because they had found employment or their children were going to school there, but longed for their old camp near the border of their homeland. ''Here I am among my own, here I can feel Palestine,'' said one man who had moved to Beirut but often still visited Rashidiyeh.

Hope and fear

It was midday as we departed to go home to Finland. Doves soared across the blue sky. A month had gone past. The sports field that we had been building together with 40 European solidarity workers was nearly finished. We printed the initials of our names in the soft surface of the cement to show symbolically that we would always be there. We hoped that the children would be able to play in peace in the field, although we knew that our wish would come true only when the Palestinians had their own country.

In the evenings we used to gather together to talk, listen to songs and dance. In the month that we were there we made many friends. Just as we were leaving, one of them hung a small piece of jewellery around my neck, a golden map of Palestine. Two years later, on 4 June 1982, Israel launched a massive assault on South Lebanon, striking by land, air and sea. The Rashidiyeh camp was the first to be destroyed. I think of all the people, my friends. Where are they? Are they alive?

The gold map around my neck is burning.

MAJ-LIS ERONEN 1982

B

A,B Rashidiyeh, October 1980

THE WAR

9 Do unto them as *unto* the Midianites; as *to* Sisera, as *to* Jabin, at the brook of Kison;

10 *Which* perished at En-dor: they became *as* dung for the earth.

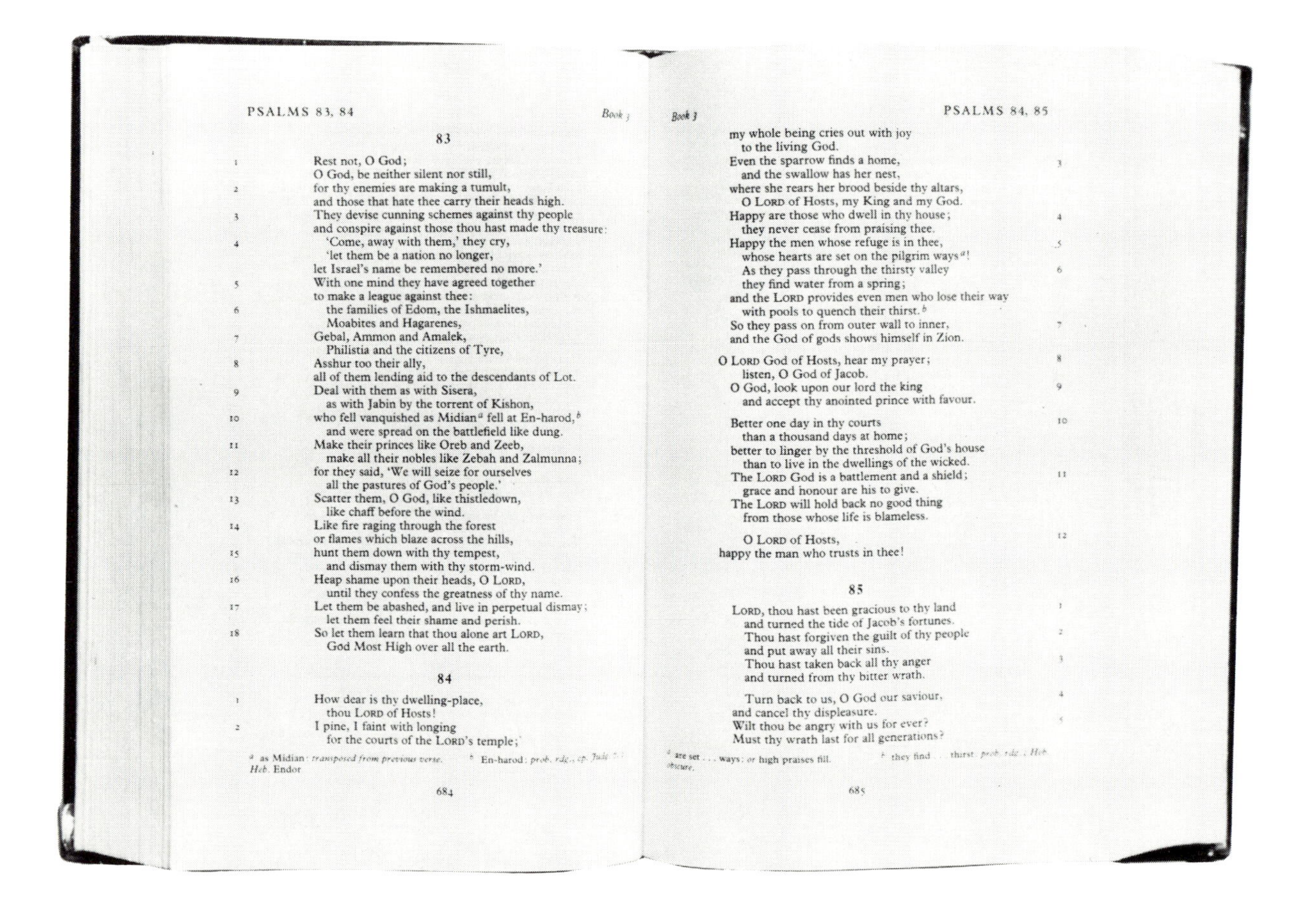

PSALMS 83, 84 *Book 3*

83

1 Rest not, O God;
O God, be neither silent nor still,
2 for thy enemies are making a tumult,
and those that hate thee carry their heads high.
3 They devise cunning schemes against thy people
and conspire against those thou hast made thy treasure:
4 'Come, away with them,' they cry,
'let them be a nation no longer,
let Israel's name be remembered no more.'
5 With one mind they have agreed together
to make a league against thee:
6 the families of Edom, the Ishmaelites,
Moabites and Hagarenes,
7 Gebal, Ammon and Amalek,
Philistia and the citizens of Tyre,
8 Asshur too their ally,
all of them lending aid to the descendants of Lot.
9 Deal with them as with Sisera,
as with Jabin by the torrent of Kishon,
10 who fell vanquished as Midian[a] fell at En-harod,[b]
and were spread on the battlefield like dung.
11 Make their princes like Oreb and Zeeb,
make all their nobles like Zebah and Zalmunna;
12 for they said, 'We will seize for ourselves
all the pastures of God's people.'
13 Scatter them, O God, like thistledown,
like chaff before the wind.
14 Like fire raging through the forest
or flames which blaze across the hills,
15 hunt them down with thy tempest,
and dismay them with thy storm-wind.
16 Heap shame upon their heads, O LORD,
until they confess the greatness of thy name.
17 Let them be abashed, and live in perpetual dismay;
let them feel their shame and perish.
18 So let them learn that thou alone art LORD,
God Most High over all the earth.

84

1 How dear is thy dwelling-place,
thou LORD of Hosts!
2 I pine, I faint with longing
for the courts of the LORD's temple;

[a] as Midian: *transposed from previous verse.* [b] En-harod: *prob. rdg., cp. Judg.* … *Heb.* Endor

684

Book 3 PSALMS 84, 85

my whole being cries out with joy
to the living God.
3 Even the sparrow finds a home,
and the swallow has her nest,
where she rears her brood beside thy altars,
O LORD of Hosts, my King and my God.
4 Happy are those who dwell in thy house;
they never cease from praising thee.
5 Happy the men whose refuge is in thee,
whose hearts are set on the pilgrim ways[a]!
6 As they pass through the thirsty valley
they find water from a spring;
and the LORD provides even men who lose their way
with pools to quench their thirst.[b]
7 So they pass on from outer wall to inner,
and the God of gods shows himself in Zion.

8 O LORD God of Hosts, hear my prayer;
listen, O God of Jacob.
9 O God, look upon our lord the king
and accept thy anointed prince with favour.

10 Better one day in thy courts
than a thousand days at home;
better to linger by the threshold of God's house
than to live in the dwellings of the wicked.
11 The LORD God is a battlement and a shield;
grace and honour are his to give.
The LORD will hold back no good thing
from those whose life is blameless.

12 O LORD of Hosts,
happy the man who trusts in thee!

85

1 LORD, thou hast been gracious to thy land
and turned the tide of Jacob's fortunes.
2 Thou hast forgiven the guilt of thy people
and put away all their sins.
3 Thou hast taken back all thy anger
and turned from thy bitter wrath.

4 Turn back to us, O God our saviour,
and cancel thy displeasure.
5 Wilt thou be angry with us for ever?
Must thy wrath last for all generations?

[a] are set . . . ways: *or* high praises fill. [b] they find . . . thirst: *prob. rdg.; Heb. obscure.*

685

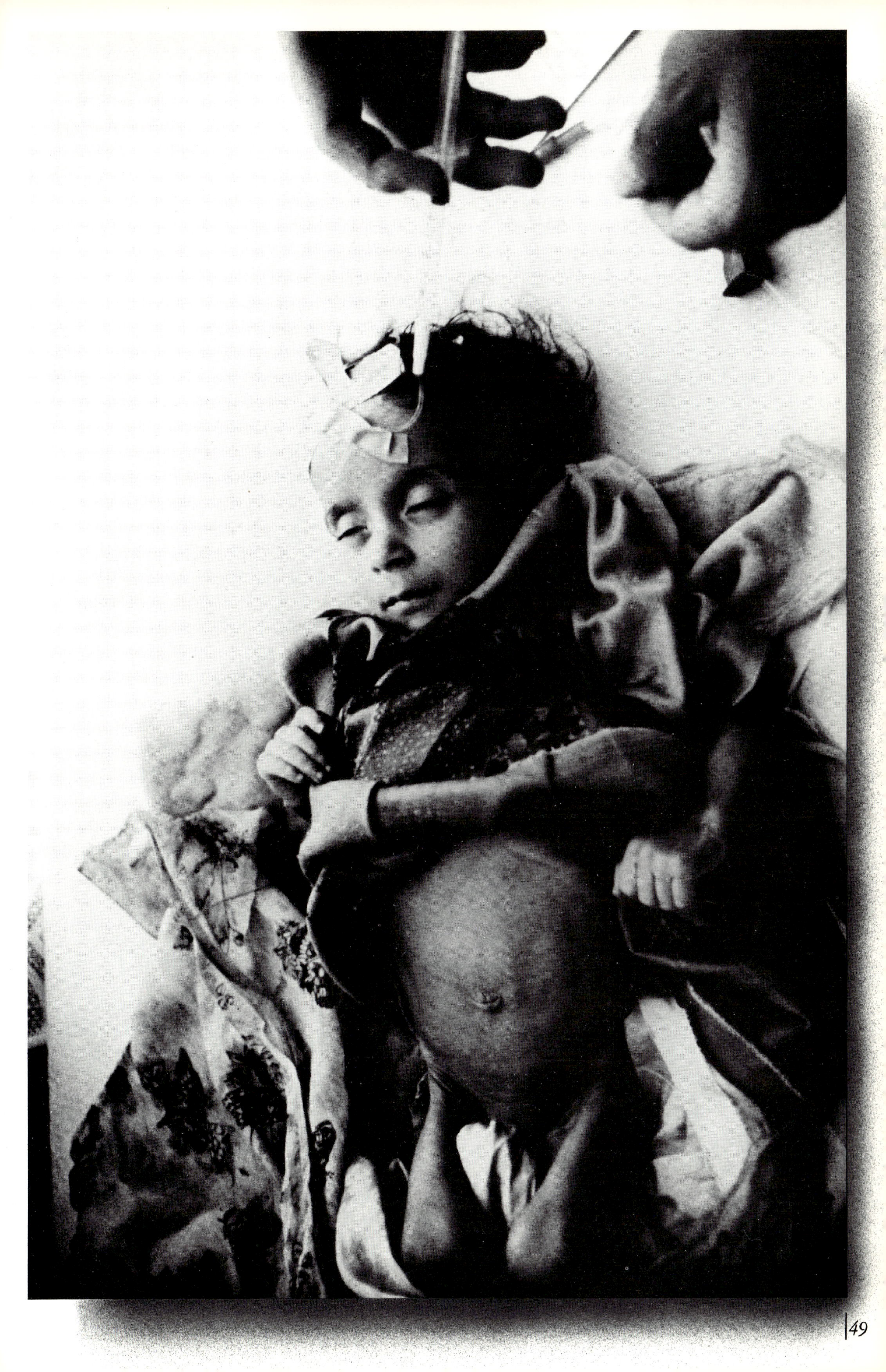

The Blooming Desert?

River Litani, tell me how you fare.
Do you still laugh? Do the frogs still laugh in your shade?
Do you still write your thoughts on the warm strand and wash them away time and time again?
Do you still compete with the sun and stumble on your own shadow?
Do you still remember me, still recall my name like yellowed leaves?
Tell me, tell me, River Litani, how you fare.

Sahban Mroueh 1978

There are places in the world where even the smallest watercourses are the nerves of life. The Bekaa Valley in South Lebanon is one such place. Its fertile soil is moistened by the River Litani.

Cultivable land is a historical and transitory phenomenon. Cultivation in Palestine is a good example of this. The country is part of the so-called Fertile Crescent, a region extending from the Tigris-Euphrates system to the Nile. It was in the oases and river valleys of this region that agriculture began in the Old World well over ten thousand years ago. With its river valleys and adjacent highlands, the plain along the eastern shore of the Mediterranean has played a central role in the development of agricultural methods.

But the Fertile Crescent also provides horrifying examples of how cultivable land can be destroyed. Rising salt levels in irrigated land as well as the erosion caused by excessive tree felling and over-grazing on slopes have long ago reduced fertile tracts to barren wastes. Conquest, war and plundering raids have time and time again destroyed what it had taken the work of generations to accomplish. Since the time of the Sumerians, Assyria and Babylon, the eastern shore of the Mediterranean has been a meeting place for seafaring and land-bound peoples, a battlefield and a melting pot. Centuries of Islamic domination beginning towards the end of the first millennium according to our Western calendar brought the region its longest period of peace, which was interrupted by the attacks of the Byzantine Empire and the plundering European brigands who have come to be known as the Crusaders. From then on, Palestine was mostly a more or less oppressed backwater of the Ottoman Empire until the 19th century, when European colonialism gradually established itself there.

The standard of agriculture varies greatly in the Middle East. Israel is the leading agricultural power in the region, with its neighbouring countries lagging far behind in productivity. There are three related reasons for this: Israel's agriculture is very modern, heavily mechanized and based on intensive use of chemicals. It is heavily export-oriented, the principal produce being fruit and vegetables. The background to this is the massive economic aid that has been flowing into the country in the decades since it was founded. Institutes of

agricultural science are of a high standard, and the country's modern universities have close contacts with research institutes and access to funds in the West (especially the US). Israel is a showpiece of the Green Revolution.

The modernization of agriculture has made it easier to thrust aside traditional methods of cultivation and old rural communities. Palestinian farmers have been driven out either through overt violence or by inventing regulations suiting the purpose. One way in which the latter method can be employed is to enact a law empowering the authorities to confiscate land that has not been tilled for a particular period and then throw its owners in jail for as long as necessary. The refugee camps in which the Palestinians live in tents in neighbouring Arab countries are the other side of the "blooming desert" coin.

The most fertile agricultural land in Palestine has been seized and is now inside the borders of Israel — a factor which has contributed to the success of Israeli agriculture. When the state was being set up, Israel seized a strip of territory along the coast and the Galilean plateau and, in 1967, the West Bank of the River Jordan. That had been the most important agricultural area in the kingdom of Jordan. The attack on Lebanon continued this tradition. As far as the Israeli government is concerned, the Litani Valley is becoming a permanently occupied province of "Northern Israel". Some 85% of Israel's water resources are used in agriculture, which gives some idea of the intensity of cultivation.

Lebanon is the other extreme. The soil is fertile and the coastal mountains make the precipitation rate quite high, but agricultural productivity is low. Continual wars have made development completely impossible; the southern parts of the country, in particular, have long lain fallow due to Israel's repeated attacks. The Litani Valley has been a desolate wasteland pockmarked with bomb and shell craters, its population forced to flee north.

How, then, does the Litani fare?

Further frightening messages have come from the banks of the river: the roar of bulldozers, the hum of pumping stations. An Israeli dream, cherished since the 1950s, is being made a reality, that of diverting the waters of the Litani to feed the irrigation network on the Galilean plateau. Like any other wealth, water, too, can be plundered — if one's greed is gross enough.

The Litani is becoming an important symbol of the recent history of Mankind. Diverting water from a river bed is like draining the blood from an animal — an act of slaughter. Our planet is small.
People must give other people the right and opportunity to live if they want to continue their existence on this planet. If this is not done, one can wave goodbye to reason and sink hope in the deepest depths of the seven seas.

YRJÖ HAILA 1982

RETURN TO SHATILA

In August
the people thought
that they could build their homes
once again.

 Sabra-Shatila, August 1982

A

A,B Sabra-Shatila, August 1982

 Sabra-Shatila, August 1982

A

B

C

D

A Burj al-Barajneh, August 1982
B,C,D,E,F Sabra-Shatila, August 1982

E

F

 Sabra-Shatila, August 1982

Beirut 1982 We did know — do we remember?

The August day was exhaustingly hot. A heat haze almost blotted out the sun in the Levantine sky. It was hot and humid, as it always is in summer in that narrow strip of Lebanon squeezed between the sea and the mountains.

The day was oppressive and oozed a looming threat, just as every day in Beirut did that summer; every day from the beginning of June onwards, a hundred in a row.

The nights, too, were oppressive, every night. Hot and humid, as though neither the heat nor the sweat would let up, nor the *angst*.

That was the night when it broke loose. A thundering roar came from behind the hills at midnight. It was followed by a whining noise for a fraction of a second, and then the roar and thunder of explosions. They went on for twenty-four hours. West Beirut was on fire, just as the besieged city had been engulfed by flames for many days.

That night the shells devoured the city everywhere. The flames licked it from house to house. It was one of the worst nights of all, the fifth of August. The city, squeezed in the bombardment of a siege, had a roof of flames above it. It was a smoking ruin the following day, and the day after that.

The five thousand dollar men

On that night, television camera crews stood silently on a hotel roof in Israeli-occupied East Beirut and filmed. They had been doing that for many nights and would continue to do it for many more.

They remained there, determinedly gripping their video cameras, only a few hundred metres from where dozens of Israeli tanks rolled in a steel chain against a defensive line that refused to be breached.

There they stood, their eyes agog. Syrian and Palestinian counter-fire whined above them from west to east. A shell fell near them. Splinters sprayed the walls. A burst of gunfire chattered from the high-rise building opposite. The others dived for what little cover the ventilation flues projecting from the flat roof provided. But the camera crews kept on filming.

During the siege of West Beirut, these cameramen, mainly representing American TV companies, gained a reputation as "legendary five thousand dollar men", prepared to go anywhere, stand anywhere. Nobody would say whether it was true or not, but it may well be that they were paid even more than the reputed sum.

Who distorted the picture?

Thanks to those people, TV screens in the West were flooded with footage showing the war in Lebanon and the bombardment of West Beirut. The picture they showed could not fail to shock. Depth was added to the scar by press photographs and articles. That picture annoyed Israeli information — or propaganda if you prefer — officials, who spoke of an information war, pro-Palestinian propaganda and distortion.

Every day, a two-thousand-dollar taxi left Beirut for the Syrian capital Damascus with a load of video cassettes. They had already been previewed and partly edited in a "field editorial office" set up in a back room at the Hotel Alexandre in Beirut. From Damascus, they were transmitted, uncensored, to the rest of the world via satellite. The same evening, the day's ration of bombardment and ruins flickered across TV screens in living rooms in Europe and America.

It is not the fault of the cameraman or videocassette if the bombardment of a metropolis is a terrible sight. It is not the fault of the eye if it sees that the civilians caught in the bombardment suffer a terrible fate.

The Israelis did not remain inactive on the information front, either. On that same night in August when the whole of West Beirut was covered in nightmarish flames, they sent a member of their parliament onto that same hotel roof to explain to foreign press representatives how they were trying to evacuate civilians. They pointed to the same places, which had been under bombardment for hours. At the same time, the tanks clanked forward and the thick-barrelled guns thundered.

Claims can be checked

During the main bombardment of West Beirut, the Israeli military command repeated time and time again that they were not firing on civilian targets, but on areas in which "terrorists" — as they have always called the Palestinians and still do — had bases.

The siege of West Beirut was an exceptional war. During the indeterminate ceasefires, press reporters could even wander freely through the ruins and across the lines to see what was going on. Civilians remained in the most heavily bombarded area, the southern part of the city, right up to the end, although many people from there fled into the crowded business centre, which was also bombarded.

The weightiest counter-argument put forward by the Israeli government and the military command was that the Palestinians had taken shelter behind the backs of the unprotected and innocent civilian population and built up their arsenal in the lee of this human wall. Nimble and egregiously expensive taxis provided an excellent means of checking the truth of this during the fragile ceasefires — fire pauses actually — that could collapse at any time.

There were weapons and fire bases, but by no means were they always located in the areas where the civilian population came under heavy bombardment. Fighters armed with light weapons were indeed all over Beirut — where even small boys were

armed, but they included Lebanese, and not just in Palestinians.

What we do not and shall not know

The Palestinians argue that their forces and weapons were there to protect the refugee camps, not to shelter in them. We know what happened in the refugee quarters of West Beirut in mid-September after the Palestinian fighters had been evacuated from the city and were no longer there to provide protection.

What happened in the refugee camps when the "terrorists" were no longer "hiding behind the backs of defenceless civilians"; how many of them were murdered — hundreds or perhaps thousands? — before the eyes of the occupiers, is something that we shall and must never be permitted to know.

Nor may we know what really happened in South Lebanon even in the early stages of the war in June and July, when the Palestinian and Lebanese fighters had retreated to West Beirut and eastern Lebanon. The majority of the Palestinian refugees remained in South Lebanon. There were not nearly so many outside eyes and ears there as there were on both sides of the battlefront in Beirut.

Free and uncensored

Hundreds of media representatives, reporters, cameramen and TV crews, flooded into Beirut during the siege. Most worked on both sides of the front, gathering information from all the parties involved.

If one had arrived in Beirut any other way than via Israel, one could work quite freely in front of the soldiers in both the western and eastern parts of the city. By contrast, those who had come via Israel were at all times accompanied by an Israeli liaison officer. Some escaped this "chaperone" by crossing over into West Beirut.

Reports and pictures were transmitted abroad by telephone, telex and telephoto or by taxi via Damascus without anybody censoring them, provided the lines worked. They usually did. Only in the last days of the siege, when the evacuation of Palestinian fighters was beginning, were communications with the whole of Beirut completely cut off. All links with both West and East Beirut were inoperative. Whether they had been deliberately severed or not was something that nobody knew.

As though by coincidence, the Israeli army had set up its own information centre on the outskirts of the city at exactly the same time. It was the only place through which information could be sent out, and there was no censorship, as there had been in Israel itself during the war. Reports flowed.

Can it happen again?

The reports scattered to the world from Beirut exuded an indignation that had never before been seen in the history of the Middle East conflict. Was it because many people told only what they had themselves seen? Is that balanced information and objectivity?

Those questions are impossible to answer. Somebody who has seen things from the inside could reply by asking where the demarcation line of impartiality runs between terror and chaos. One can also ask how long the world will remember Beirut — and if it can happen again.

HEIKKI ÄLLI 1982

Letter from exile

A kiss for you and — salutations
What else should I say
Where to begin and where to end
Time flows away without restriction
And all I have in exile stored:
A loaf of bread, mouldy and hard
A copybook full of disappointments
And longing for my beloved
Where shall I begin

All that was said
Or will be said
Could not return me home
Nor will it bring rain
Or grow feathers on an aging bird

A message in Listener's Mail.
"Tell her I am well"
I tell the sparrow:
"Do not forget, if you're ever there
Tell her I am well"

Well o well
I still can see
The sky is not moonless
My clothes are not yet torn
Although there are patches — here and there
But it's all right now

I am now grown — over twenty
The burdens of life I shoulder like men
I work in a tavern, as dishwasher
And coffee maker
You should see me Ma
A smile on my face
For the customer's sake!

I also smoke and stand at the corner
To speak with the girls

Like other young men
Life is unbearable without women.

I am well
I have a loaf of bread
And some vegetables

I heard on the radio
Messages of the exiles
They all concurred, without dissent:
"We are quite well."
No one has said: "I am distressed"
Or "It's wretched here".

How's my father?
Does he still pray?
Does he love children, the land and olives
As he always did?
And how are my brothers
Did they graduate?
Are they teachers now?
Like my father used to say

Do you know what grieves me sometimes
Suppose I fell ill
Will the night pity me
Will the tree under which I fell
Recognize my body as that of a man
And give it protection from hungry beasts

My dear Mother
Why did I write these letters
There is no mail
The land, sea, and air are blocked
And you all might be dead
Or perhaps alive without address

Should we go on
No country — no home — no flag — no address

MAHMOUD DARWISH

EVACUATION

The fighters left in August
Yearning for their loved ones
The families stayed behind
dreading September

FEBRUARY 1983

The rains of winter can extinguish hope
We're not going to live in the tents
we'll simply burn them.
We won't abandon our houses,
even though we can't repair them.
At least there's some trace
a slab or wall, a remnant of roof.
We may still have a bit of bread to eat
but we've no news of our nearest ones.
A letter
from the concentration camp — a ray of light
Two months of longing in eight censored lines
you're alive, at least

With the Spring resistance will dawn again.

الفاتحة
ضريح المرحوم الحاج
سليم شرور
ولد في قرية علما قضاء
صفد فلسطين
سنة ١٨٧٥ وتوفي يوم
بسم الله الرحمن الرحيم
يا ايتها النفس المطمئنة
ارجعي الى ربك راضية
مرضية فادخلي في عبادي
وادخلي جنتي
كل نفس ذائقة الموت

A

B

A,B
Rashidiyeh,
February 1983

INTERNATIONAL COMMITTEE
GENEVA

Rashidiyeh, February 1983

Israel seized the Gaza Strip from Egypt in the Six-Day War of 1967, and has continued to occupy it ever since. Even before this time it housed many refugee camps: after the State of Israel was founded in 1948 people from numerous towns and villages were deported there.

The Occupation in 1967 reduced the significance of the border and many Palestinians now had their first chance of meeting relatives or seeking out what was left of their homes in what had since become Israel. Majdi Saadallah's family were planning to visit their home village ten years ago. His father was killed in 1967 by the Israelis as they shelled the villages and camps after capturing Gaza.

Return to the old village

This is the story of my grandfather.

My uncle said that it's possible to go and see our old village. He was about 20 years old when he left it in 1948 and he was eager to see it again. For him our village represents his childhood and part of his youth. It is a lost paradise to some extent, but it is real.

For me it is a cultural symbol, a pilgrimage, but for my grandfather — I'll talk about that later.

We went to my grandfather and told him. He did not resist, but neither did he readily accept the idea. We decided to go the next day.

We had left Khan Younis early in the morning, and I sat beside him. He was silent and when we crossed the border line (is there any border line?) my uncle became talkative and eager to recite the names of all the places we passed. My grandfather, however, was silent, watching everything. I couldn't see his eyes, but he was nervous.

After a while my uncle announced we were near the village, but we saw only green fields around us. We spent about an hour going from one place to another looking for the village, asking people we met about it, but they knew nothing. (We discovered later that it had been given a new Hebrew name.)

Suddenly my grandfather asked the driver to stop. He opened the door, got out and sat beside the car. He touched the sand and examined it, then stood up and told us to follow him, saying, ''I'll lead you to the village now.''

We followed him and he said to me, ''I'll show you your house.''

The place was empty, but everything was fresh in his mind. ''Our house was here,'' he said. Then he mentioned every house in the village. He indicated an empty spot: ''Your father used to play there.'' I was very eager to see my father's playground and other reminders of his childhood. My grandfather then suggested we go and see the well. Finding the well still there, we drank some of the water and bottled some. Grandfather then said: ''Let us go and see the cemetery.'' Parts of it had been destroyed, but my grandfather found his father's tomb and recited some parts of the Quran that his soul might rest in peace, and for the others also. He went to the mosque, only to find they had destroyed it.

When we returned to Khan Younis he was silent. He went straight home and fell sick; he was bedridden for a long time. We gave the water to my grandmother. She allowed no-one to drink it and kept it for more than two months. She used to drink a few drops every day before her morning prayers.

I understand now that when my grandfather went to his village and discovered that they had destroyed it, that destroyed him. He recognized his own defeat; but I was surprised because he had been able to touch his own soil and discover that mystical relationship between man and earth.

How can I escape the image of that village? It haunts and follows me everywhere.

MAJDI SAADALLAH

AL-SIT ZEYNAB

Through the canvas the summer sun burns things to a cinder
In winter blue frost turns the tent into an ice-box
The desert wind, freezing rain
The tent our only shelter
The first memory of refugee childhood,
The final sensation of refugee life.

The Middle East — the background to the struggle

Time is on the side of the Palestinians

Few places on our planet have witnessed so many wars as the Middle East. A coincidence? Are the peoples who inhabit the Middle East bellicose by nature? Are special features of the local culture or religions behind the conflicts? An examination of the Middle East's history soon shows that the answer to all of those questions is "no".

The Middle East's wars have been brought there from outside. They have not been the creation of the peoples living in the region. Those peoples have, nevertheless, had to bear the greatest burden, because it is they who have waged the various wars, knowingly or unknowingly on the orders of powerful outside forces. On a horizon obscured by the dust clouds of the battle, it has been difficult to discern the major lines of history.

Wars have been brought to the Middle East by powers seeking hegemony over the region, for motives that have varied in the course of the millennia. The conquest of the region by its earliest colonial masters, the Romans, was motivated by hunger for territory in which to plant colonialists from the overpopulated mother country, whereas by the middle of the present millennium the need had changed to that of subjugating the peasants there. They, too, had become necessary to the economy of the mother country.

The background to every endeavour to subjugate the Middle East reveals that the area has been affected by a unique set of factors and features peculiar to the period in question. One must be careful to avoid oversimplification and not allow details nor side intrigues to distract one's attention from the essential. There has been far too much readiness to brand the conflicts of the Middle East as religious wars. It cannot be denied that religious intrigues play a role in a region so central to three of the world's major religions — Christianity, Islam and Judaism — and religious concepts probably still have a greater influence on the formation of public opinion in the Middle East than in other parts of the world, but it can also be shown that nearly a thousand years ago the Crusaders' campaigns to safeguard the Sacred Tomb had strongly economic motives. Religion served as the justification for conquest. The same has applied in later times; the cause of the conflict has not been a religion nor religions, but they have very often been the means and trigger by which wars have been ignited and waged.

The colonial masters strengthen their grip

When one examines the events of recent decades, it does not take long to find the reasons for the interest that has been focused on the Middle East. In the early part of our century, and especially after the Second World War, oil became a very essential raw material. Roughly two-thirds of the known oil reserves in the non-socialist world are in the Middle East. And time and time again, the needs and wishes of the local peoples have been buried in the sand in the struggle for control of that oil.

Since the end of the Second World War, the United States has become the most influential outside power in the region. On several occasions, its formulations of policy programmes on the region have included the point that Middle East oil is vital to the United States and its allies. Those formulations have not made any mention of how vital peace and secure social development are to the peoples of the region.

There is no denying the strategic importance of the Middle East. It stands at one of the world's major crossing points, where Europe, Asia and Africa meet. Every commodity from loads of spices on camels' backs to crude oil in supertankers has passed through the region that has straddled some of the world's most important trade routes since the dawn of history.

The opening of the Suez Canal in the latter half of the 19th century vastly increased the importance of the Middle East. An unprecedented wave of colonial expansion was under way and the canal immediately became an important route for goods transported between the mother countries and the colonies. Britain and France — then the leading colonial powers — had been struggling for possession of the Middle East since the early years of the century.

The present core area of the Middle East conflict — Palestine — played a central role in these schemes. It was one of the areas close to the Suez Canal that were considered necessary to control in order to safeguard possession of the waterway. Throughout the 19th century, the British strengthened their positions in the area, which was still under Turkish suzerainty; formal assertion of colonial mastery was postponed for tactical reasons.

The Arab states in the region, which had been under Turkish rule since the 16th century, expected to become independent when Turkey's power collapsed, but instead of independence they got new colonial masters. Britain and France divided the region between them when they inherited it from Turkey after the First World War. However, the world was no longer the same one in which colonialist states carved up continents between them. The Soviet Russia had come into being in 1917, and the effects of the October Revolution were immediately felt far beyond the borders of Russia. They were felt particularly strongly in colonially-ruled countries close to Russia. By the 1920s, the struggle against colonial rule had reached an unprecedented level. Britain's and France's plans to divide the region up between them were a century too late; the peoples of the Middle East would no longer submit to colonial conquest without a fight.

The British and French had planned to divide the region up neatly and without too much noise. The instrument was secret diplomacy, which led to the Sykes-Picot Agreement, in which it was agreed which areas should go to whom.

The agreement was signed while the First World War was still raging and the Middle East still under Turkish control. At the same time as the British and French were haggling over the spoils, however, they had given completely different promises to the emerging independence movements in the region. In order to secure these movements' support in the war against Turkey, the two colonial powers promised them independence. The Russian Revolution provided an obstacle to implementation of those promises. Czarist Russia had been one of the guarantors of the Sykes-Picot Agreement, and that secret document was published in Russia after the revolution. The revelation of Britain's and France's real intentions sparked off a very strong anti-colonial movement in the Middle East and these two countries were no longer to conduct the carve-up as originally envisaged.

Putting people against people

At the same time that it was planning the division of the region, Britain had also carried out another diplomatic move that was to have serious consequences for the security of the Middle East. Determining the fate of a region that belonged to her neither formally nor de facto, Britain promised the Zionists that a "national homeland" would be established in Palestine.

Britain needed Palestine as an important part of her empire, but did not consider it an enticing place in which to transplant her own colonialists. However, she knew that in order to be able to suppress resistance by the indigenous population she needed a population group loyal to her in the region. Her attention turned to the Jews. Since the latter part of the 19th century, Zionist organizations had been actively looking for a place in which the national movement that had emerged among the Jews could establish a state of its own.

Palestine was not by any means the only territory considered by the Zionist movement. Places as far apart as German East Africa and Argentina had been examined. On its own, the Zionist movement could never have achieved its goal; it needed the support of a major colonial power. Promises given and calculations made during the First World War began altering the political situation in the Middle East in the years immediately after the signing of the armistice.

Althought the basis for implementation of the Sykes-Picot Agreement collapsed, Britain and France nevertheless managed to divide the region between them. This was done under the auspices of the League of Nations, the organization set up by the victors after the First World War. France was given a Mandate to administer Syria and Lebanon; Britain, Iraq, Transjordan and Palestine. The Middle East had again gained a new strategic importance, because a drive was on to smother the young Soviet state in its cradle through a series of interventionist wars and the region provided a springboard for assaults against the southern parts of Russia. The colonial powers strengthened their grip on the Middle East.

The period between the world wars revealed an increasingly more obvious crisis in old-style colonialism. As early as the 1930s, the colonial masters began to encounter mounting difficulties in the Middle East, Western Asia and North Africa. In her attempts to colonize Morocco, France ran into well-organized and powerful resistance by the local tribes. This culminated in the establishment of the Rif Republic in the liberated areas of the country in the early years of the 1920s. Colonizing Algeria proved extremely difficult, and a freedom struggle of national proportions was waged against Syria's new colonial masters in the 1920s.

The British encountered growing problems in Egypt in the early 1920s. The crisis of their colonial system deepened also in Persia and Afghanistan, which proved impossible to conquer by force of arms. Events in the Arabian peninsula, where an independent Saudi kingdom emerged in the 1920s, were also disturbing from the British point of view. Colonial administration was fiercely resisted in Iraq.

In the Palestinian area, the local population's resistance to the mandate erupted into a wave of liberation struggles in the 1920s and 1930s. The overall situation there was further complicated by an influx of Jewish immigrants. The Zionist movement remained loyal to its colonial masters at first, but the situation changed as soon as it believed it had gained enough strength to oppose the British presence in Palestine and campaign for an independent Jewish state.

On the whole, the situation was proving very difficult for either the British or the French to control. Both military power and political means were used in an effort to dam the nationalist movement. Britain, in particular, tried to disguise the continuation of her influence in the cloak of independent kingdoms. Members of feudal dynasties considered loyal to Britain were installed as monarchs of Middle Eastern countries. An "independent" kingdom of Egypt was created in the early 1920s. Representatives of families that supported Britain in her quest for supremacy over the Arabian peninsula were installed as kings of Transjordan and Iraq. This background should be borne in mind, because by operating in this way the British were able to ensure the continuation of their diplomatic influence in spite of the threatening changes that were taking place.

In the years immediately before the Second World War, the strategic importance of the Middle East was reflected in the intensity of diplomatic manoeuvres concerning the region. Germany tried to gain political allies or at least facilities as part of her preparations for an attack on the Soviet Union. Now, too, promises of independence were the means chosen. Britain and France also made similar promises. All the promises were just as false as those made earlier and the disappointment they engendered caused an even stronger eruption once the war had ended. The British and French response to this resistance was an increase in terror.

However, the Second World War had changed the situation in the Middle East. The United States was becoming a greater influence in the region than the old colonial powers, Britain and France, and prepared to accept responsibility for keeping the Middle East, i.e. its oil, within the Western sphere of influence. Britain's mandate to administer Palestine was about to expire, but this did not mean that Britain was prepared to abandon her positions either in Palestine or anywhere else in the Middle East. The transfer of power was a bitter pill for Britain to swallow. Negotiations between Britain and the United States in 1945 and 1946 failed to achieve a solution to the Palestinian problem. The United States had come out more and more openly in support of Jewish demands for independence, whilst the British stuck to their rights in Palestine.

The cuckoo's egg

The present shape of things in the Middle East was beginning to emerge. Britain threw the situation that had arisen in relation to the mandate into the lap of the United Nations. The background to this featured several important changes: in the course of the mandate period (officially from 1923 to 1948), the population structure in Palestine altered dramatically, with the Jews increasing their share from about 12 per cent to slightly over 30 per cent. At the same time, land that had been in Arab possession had been consistently bought up and placed at the Jews' disposal. The Jewish community had been able to create a "state within a state" and build up a strong army. The British were confronted with the inescapable fact that the young cuckoo was preparing to push its foster parents out of the nest and to ensure its own growth by making conditions for the Palestinians virtually impossible.

From the very beginning, the Palestinian problem was a very complex and multi-faceted one, although from the historical perspective it was clearly a creation of colonialism — something that had been brought into the region from outside. The Jewish and Arab movements against British rule contained elements of anti-colonial struggle. Tactical disputes between Britain and the United States became apparent in the Palestine question, especially when it was debated in the United Nations; in the final analysis, both powers had very similar designs on the natural wealth of the region.

The United Nations' handling of the Palestine question ended on 29 November, 1947, when a resolution on the territory was passed. This had been preceded in May of the same year by the appointment of a special UN commission charged with the task of finding a solution to the problem. The commission agreed unanimously that Britain's rule under the mandate should end as soon as possible, but not on how this was to be accomplished. A majority supported the creation of two independent states — one Jewish and one Palestinian, whilst a minority favoured a federal state.

The decision to partition Palestine was taken after a vote in the UN General Assembly, with about two-thirds voting for partitition and one third against. The countries that abstained included Britain, whose behaviour during the UN's handling of the matter showed quite clearly that she was still not prepared to relinquish the mandate voluntarily. Britain's motive in abstaining was to leave herself free hands. Both the United States and Britain were engaged in a feverish search for a solution that would safeguard their own interests in the Middle East.

After the decision to partition Palestine had been taken, diplomatic manoeuvres affecting the fate of the country accelerated. New plans were pulled out of the bag. Britain executed an unexpected move in announcing that she would relinquish her mandate already on 15 May, 1948 — the UN resolution had called for this to happen by 1 August. Behind the British move was the obvious calculation that in co-operation with those Arab states with which she had close relations she would be able to regain her position in Palestine by force of arms. For her part, the United States calculated that, having failed to gain control over Palestine in the form of a UN mandate, it would be in her best interests to act through the Jewish community there.

We know what those intrigues led to: The first large-scale military engagement between Israel and the surrounding Arab states immediately after Israel had proclaimed herself independent on 15 May, 1948. The war was a defeat for Britain and those Arab states that had gone to war. Israel gained control over considerably more territory than had been apportioned to her in the UN resolution. The foundation of the Palestinian state was postponed indefinitely and nearly a million Palestinians were forced to flee their native land. The war strengthened Israel's position and put the seal on the United States' tightening grip on the Middle East.

Decades of war

Four major conflicts have raged in the Middle East since the 1948 war — in 1956, 1967, 1973 and 1982. A state of war has existed continuously in the Middle East since the foundation of Israel. Viewed from the Palestinian perspective, the assault has proceeded in a very planned fashion. Israel has also targeted the places to which the largest concentrations of Palestinian refugees have been driven.

Through wars and threats of violence, the Middle East has been kept in uncertainty for four decades. It has been in the interests of imperialism to prevent stabilization of the situation in the region. In this part of the world, too, the forces opposing each other since the Second World War have, in the final analysis, been a national liberation movement — in this case the Arab people's struggle for greater political and economic independence — and imperialist opposition to this movement's goals.

Israel's arms are always aimed not only at Palestine, but also at the particular Arab country that at any given time most clearly pursues policies opposed to imperialist aspirations in the Middle East. When Egypt was spearheading the Arab liberation struggle, she was the target. Both Iraq and Syria have suffered vengeance. The Arab countries have been pressured and fragmented. Difficulties in creating a united Arab front stem largely from deliberate and consistent efforts to prevent progress towards unity. Nor has the internal development of the Arab countries been left to those countries themselves to decide.

A basic prerequisite for the achievement of permanent peace in the Middle East is that the legal rights of the exiled Palestinian Arab people be safeguarded. Denying this fact can correspond only to the interests of those forces that need wars in the Middle East. In the situation after the 1973 war, the possibility of a broadly-based negotiation process seemed to be emerging in the region, but Camp David ended this by excluding even the UN from the talks. Once again, the Middle East had been steered towards war.

The extremely warlike face of the Camp David "peace process" was revealed in all its horribleness by events in the summer of 1982. Can one expect to achieve peace through blood and the sword? The events in Lebanon that summer showed above all how free Camp David had left Israel to continue the policy of aggression that she had been pursuing for decades. The ruthlessness with which Israel acted against the Palestinians sprang from the soil of Camp David, which the United States was instrumental in creating.

To the Palestinians, the Camp David process has meant a difficult stretch on the long road of evacuation. But this people, which is struggling for its very existence, has managed to overcome even the most difficult obstacles that it has encountered in the past. The Palestinian state goes on. Time is on the side of the Palestinians.

PERTTI MULTANEN
June 1983

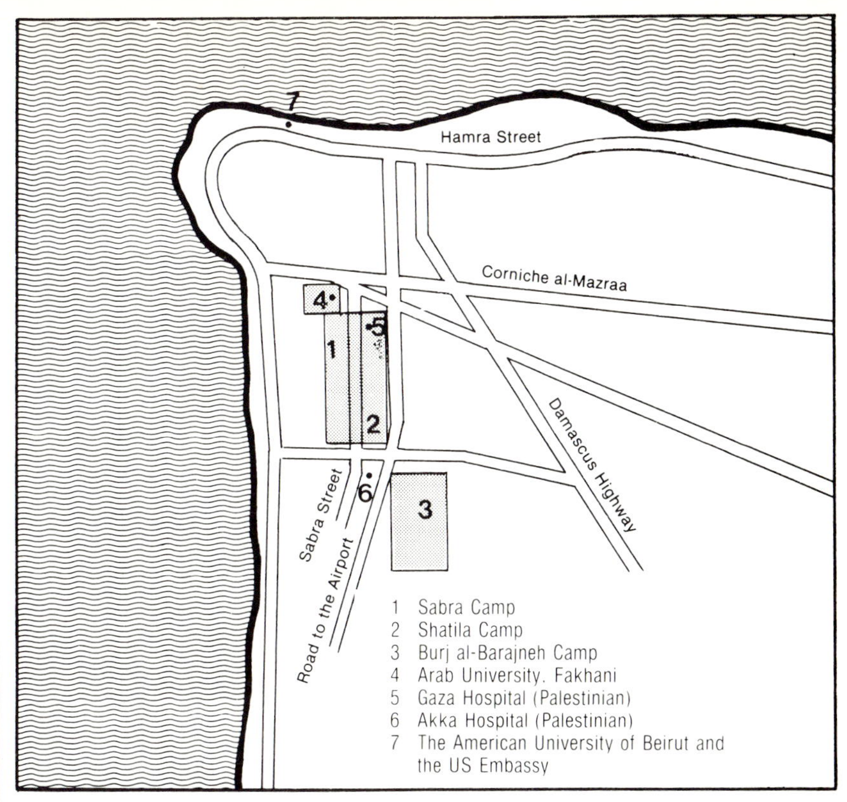

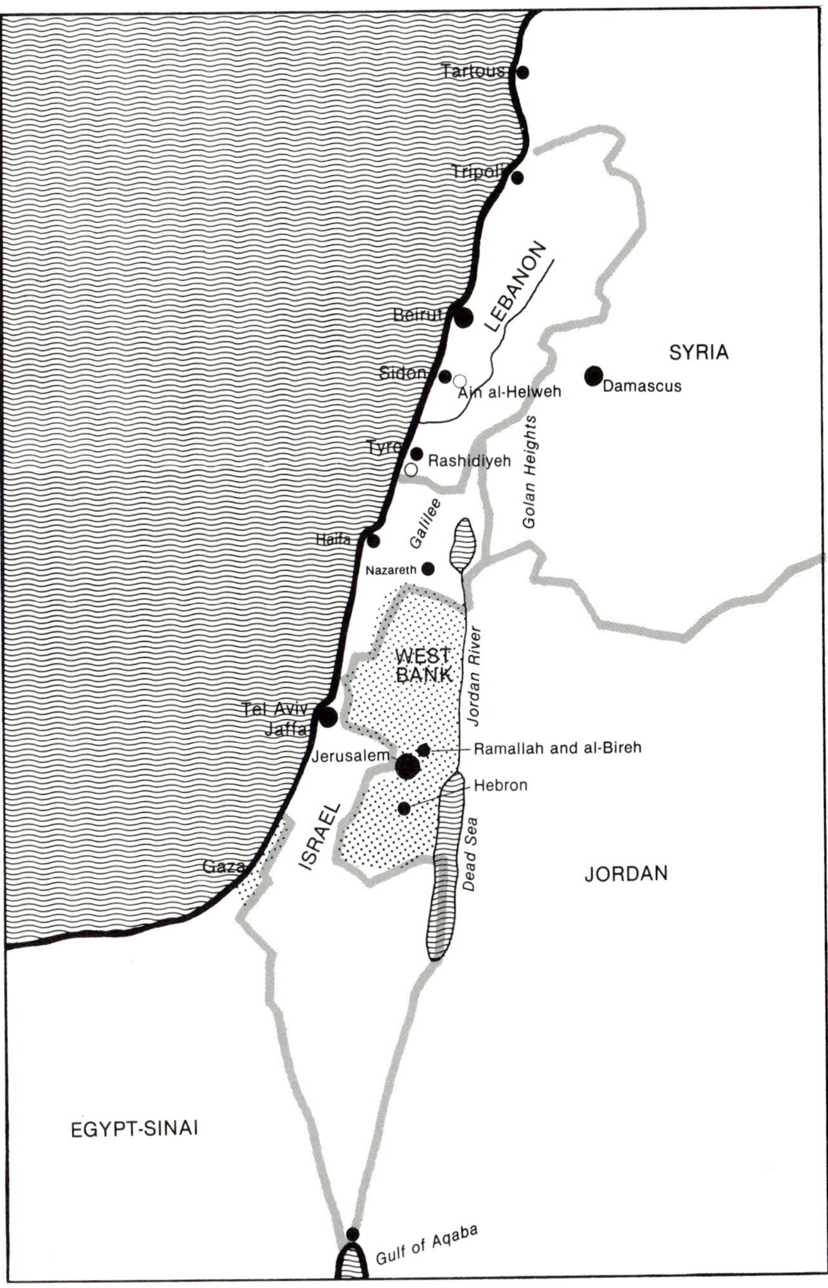

Recommended reading:

Frangi, Abdallah, *The PLO and Palestine* (Zed Books Ltd., 1983)
Nassib, Selim and Tisdall, Caroline, *Beirut Frontline Story* (Pluto Press, 1983)
Rodinson, Maxime, *Israel and the Arabs* (Penguin Books, 1982)
Jansen, Michael, *The Battle of Beirut: Why Israel Invaded Lebanon* (Zed Books Ltd., 1982)
Metzger, J., Orth, M., and Sterzing, S., *This Land is Our Land: The West Bank Under Israeli Occupation* (Zed Books Ltd., 1983)